BLOOD, DEBT & FEARS

BLOOD, DEBT & FEARS

Cartoons of the first half of the last half of the Bush Administration

JEFF DANZIGER

Foreword by Jeffrey Frank

STEERFORTH PRESS • HANOVER, NEW HAMPSHIRE

FOR THE TROOPS

For information about permission to reproduce
selections from this book, write to:
Steerforth Press L.C., 25 Lebanon Street,
Hanover, New Hampshire 03755

Danziger cartoons are syndicated by
Cartoonists and Writers Syndicate
and distributed by

The New York Times
SYNDICATE

www.nytimages.com

The Library of Congress has cataloged this volume.

ISBN 10: 1-58642-112-3
ISBN 13: 978-1-58642-112-0

FIRST EDITION

Book design by Peter Holm, Sterling Hill Productions

Peter De Vries in *The Tunnel of Love* described one of his characters, a cartoonist, as "a third-rate artist in whom a first-rate gagman was trying to claw his way out." A funny line – De Vries was a funny man – but it is also a reminder that our best editorial cartoonists have to manage the complete hat trick: that is, they must be funny, but also draw brilliantly, and simultaneously deal with the unrelentingly unfunny news of our time. It's a rare and mysterious talent, and the best of them, like Jeff Danziger, do all of this while showing almost no respect for the decent opinions of mankind. Who but a cartoonist would bury King Fahd of Saudi Arabia in a coffin that looks just like an oil drum? Or would portray a religious leader – say Pat Robertson – like a buzzard, and in fact a buzzard who gets socked with a clump of bird shit?

It's also true that mankind doesn't seem to have much respect for the decent opinions of cartoonists. Fewer newspapers want them on staff; they're an inconvenient luxury, not only demanding salaries for their labor, but annoying those subscribers who manage to see infusions of racism and general intolerance in just about every sort of drawing. And after all, it's much easier just to buy a cartoonist's stuff from a syndicate, where you only have to deal with slick paper or PDF files. I once worked for a small Gannett operation in upstate New York, and only lately have I realized that we were in league with the future of the newspaper business. We paid, if I recall, about $7.50 a week for the right to reprint the work of artists like Pat Oliphant and Jeff MacNelly, and of course it was risk-free and pretty much cost-free too; if readers didn't like something that we printed,

King Fahd Mourned

well, readers could just call the syndicate, and if we got impatient with an artist, we could always "hire" another one, or even another two. And because we were a one-paper town — Gannett adored and still adores one-paper towns, and there are many more of them today than there used to be — the price we paid never seemed to increase. I recall a time when one syndicate informed us that they going to raise the rate of some popular columnist by a dollar a week, and our response was a cancellation. Oops.

That's what makes the work of artists like Jeff Danziger — fearless, tireless, perpetually outraged — all the more remarkable. So far as I know, none of these people are getting rich, and yet that seems to do nothing to slow them down. Perhaps that makes them push harder, in more of a snit. The state of the world, somehow, works

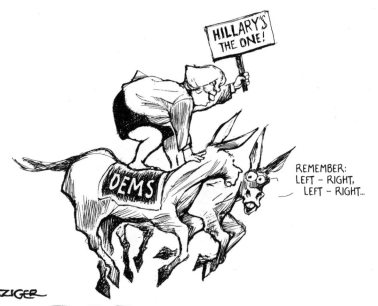

HILLARY'S THE ONE!

DEMS

REMEMBER: LEFT – RIGHT, LEFT – RIGHT...

DANZIGER

its charms, and as a result we see them portraying a White House where the staffers slink around (after Bible study, of course) with knives sticking out of their backs, or we see a "war president" who claims that proud title, just like Lincoln and F.D.R. did, because thousands of American soldiers have died — never mind that it's in a war that's being fought in a time and place and with a rationale of his choosing. Or we see the vice president peering dementedly out of his bunker. And New York's ambitious junior senator straddling two donkeys whose cadence is "left-right, left-right."

Our best cartoonists tend to be obsessed, too; they just can't seem to let go of certain subjects. Is America's industrial strength being hollowed out by cheap imports from China? Are soldiers being killed and maimed and then ignored when they're veterans and need medical help and rehabilitation? Is the commander-in-chief an idiot, or is he just playing one when he speaks from the Oval Office, the better to please his base? There is no way to express such intemperate views without sounding a bit shrill, and yet opinions in American newspapers are rarely expressed with anything approaching shrillness. Rather, judiciousness and sobriety are the form, and the unspoken rule is to maintain respect for the office. Cartoonists, who aren't judicious or respectful, have an almost primal, shamanistic role; they make us laugh when sometimes all we want to do is scream. Another Danziger collection is a happy invitation to join in and howl.

Jeffrey Frank, the author of *The Columnist* and *Bad Publicity*, is a senior editor at *The New Yorker*.

Blood, Oil, Fears, and Debt

We are now in the fourth year of the war to revenge ourselves on someone for the attacks September 11, 2001. For Americans who served in the late great Vietnam War, the rhyme of history has a morbid humor to it. So far we have seen almost everything that happened in Vietnam repeated, a splintered mirror of the past, but this time speeded up. The initial heroism of the march on Baghdad to the present bloody quagmire has happened in half the time it took Lyndon Johnson and Richard Nixon in the sixties and seventies.

They don't teach much about Vietnam in U.S. high schools. The school year, which seems to get ever shorter, runs out before the teacher gets to recent events. Modern history might include Churchill's "Blood, Toil, Tears, and Sweat" speech, but most students think it's a rock group. The point of the Second World War was that we won.

There are some wars you're better off not knowing about. Young American troops, for the most part, don't see the historical parallels between the early victories in Southeast Asia and the early victories in Baghdad. Nor do they see the similarities between the tiger cages of Con Son Island and the torture and abuses at Guantanamo and Abu Ghraib. They don't recognize the parallels between Robert McNamara's stubborn predictions of ultimate success and Donald Rumsfeld's increasingly stubborn defense of his own arguments. We leave no child behind.

In this present war, all the errors and horrors we saw in the Vietnamese jungles and mountain stumble on top of each other. Things happen faster in the barren wastes around Fallujah and Kandahar than they did in the triple canopy jungle on Nui Ba Den and the sodden paddies around Can Tho. It took many years for the legitimately decent efforts of U.S. Special Forces to gain the trust the South Vietnamese. And many years more for the conflict to degenerate into a struggle by the U.S. Army to simply take and hold territory. In Afghanistan, this same degeneration took mere months. Our political leaders rapidly segued from reasonable conjecture about weapons of mass destruction to outright misrepresentation and fraud.

Like Lyndon Johnson, Mr. Bush has retreated from reality as the evidence of his mistakes mounted. Like Nixon he has invoked larger issues, more flamboyant abstractions, and sought sympathy for himself personally as an unappreciated and uncredited savior. There are times when you half expect him to claim he has a secret plan for getting out of Iraq. This is a horrible thing to have to witness. Mr. Bush is probably a nice guy and would have made a pleasant junior high school assistant principal. As a war leader, however, he is an clumsy agent of disaster, and a cold-hearted enemy of promise. Even more sordid is his awkward, teleprompted religiousness that all but out-Gods the insanity of the bloody-minded mullahs of Islamic fundamentalism. The killing goes on. Neither side will admit being wrong, or having made mistakes, or having failed to provide a good life for its adherents. It reminds one of the Bourbon kings who, in their centuries of reign, were described as having learned nothing and forgotten nothing. While humanity spends lives and money on settling these essentially unimportant political feuds,

the real problems of the planet go unattended, largely ignored. And it all seems to be happening faster and faster.

In times so dreadful, cartoons may easily be dismissed, at least in this country, as less than sufficiently serious. Americans usually think of cartoons as having been invented by Walt Disney, their appeal depending on either cuteness or stupidity. But if done well, a cartoon is more art than idea. And in these accelerating times, a drawing is useful because it's quicker. A drawing does one thing better than the written word: it leaps into the consciousness and sets up shop before you know it. (Black and white drawings leap quicker than color, by the way.) Thus, or at least thus-it-is-hoped, drawings get to people who don't have the inclination or the time to read a series of periodic sentences arranged in an inescapable expository order of support. Not surprisingly, the best political art is often found in posters, barking a warning at passersby. A writer can spend many column inches delineating how much money the Bush administration has wasted and how future generations will be saddled by the weight of this debt. The cartoonist can have him delivering an anvil to the cradle. One form doesn't obviate the need for the other. If you react to the cartoon, you'll seek the details in the text, and if you have been reading the text, the next cartoon will be that much more effective. And the dessert, the reward for having finished all the succotash of the news, is that you might even be amused.

I am, as Gerald Ford used to say, "acutely aware" that a tendentious gloom has crept into my second collection of drawings about the Bush

The Babysitter

DANZIGER

Congressman Jefferson (D-La.) Explains the Ninety Grand in His Freezer

administration. There are more soldiers spouting mordant comments as the bullets hiss by. There are more cartoons of wreckage and misery. There is more incipient disaster and threatening risk. There is an explosion in the warscape on the cover, and several more such explosions throughout the pages. All in all an unpleasant collection. I do apologize, as we say these days, if anyone is offended.

But here's the good news. There *is* comic relief every so often. At least once a week we are saved from our depression by the antics of people like Pat Robertson, a man God has sent to cheer us up and lift us from various despondent sloughs. Pat truly is a godsend. And we must thank him profusely, lest he think we don't appreciate his threatening to shoot Hugo Chavez, or leg press two thousand pounds with the help of his herbal power supplement. And on the left we must thank Congressman William Jefferson, who kept his incoming bribe money in his freezer.

Of course, on further reflection, when you realize that Pat Robertson and William Jefferson are the lone rays of sunshine amongst the crepuscular clouds of conflict you might just get all gloomy again.

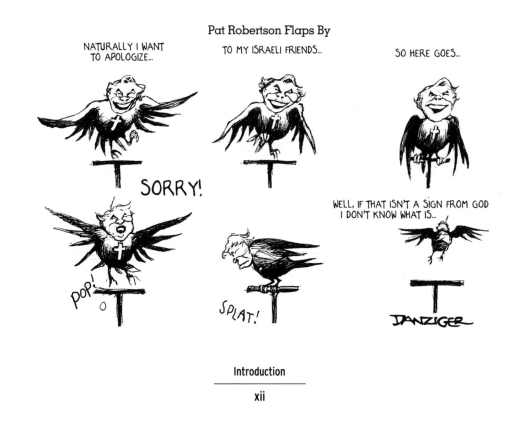

Pat Robertson Flaps By

NATURALLY I WANT TO APOLOGIZE...

TO MY ISRAELI FRIENDS...

SO HERE GOES...

SORRY!

POP!

SPLAT!

WELL, IF THAT ISN'T A SIGN FROM GOD I DON'T KNOW WHAT IS...

DANZIGER

In Bluest Vermont

Our friends at the Club for Growth waste their valuable time slagging the poor little state of Vermont as a ". . . tax-hiking, government-spending, sushi-eating, latte-drinking, Volvo-driving Hollywood freak show."

The secret of success in America's third century.

March 12, 2004

The government sends out tapes of fake reports that look like independently produced news. Some stations actually run them.

Speaker Hastert and Congressman Hyde, safe and warm in Washington, and having had a good big breakfast, plus a mid-morning snack, give their considered opinion of the Spanish people...

Terrorists blow up morning commuter trains in Madrid. While accusations are flying, our own heroes, Dennis Hastert and Henry Hyde, start calling people names.

March 19, 2004

L. Paul Bremer, having run out of mistakes and misjudgements, decides that sovereignity is the better part of valor.

April 5, 2004

Ah, Remember the Good Old Days?

when the only person running around
Washington with his hair on fire
was that goof Richard A. Clarke?

Mr. Clarke's frantic warnings about US operations in the Middle East are
gaining new fans in the White House.

March 29, 2004

Smoking Is Outlawed in Pubs in Ireland

Meanwhile, in most of Europe, smoking is under attack. The Irish discover that there are worse things than the odor of tobacco.

May 29, 2004

Radical cleric Muqtada al-Sadr is fingered by Mr. Wolfowitz. If we can only get him, everything will turn out fine. The Pentagon report says so.

April 7, 2004

The 9/11 Commission calls in the always impressive Dr. Rice. At one point she nearly answers a question.

April 7, 2004

9

Shiites and Sunnis Are Joining Together to Fight US Occupation

SO... BUSH WAS RIGHT!

YES! HE IS A UNITER, NOT A DIVIDER!

DANZIGER

Sunnis discover that the enemy, the Shiites, of their enemy, the United States, is their friend. This effect is fortunately only temporary.

Abdul Khan, Father of the Pakistan A-Bomb, May Have Fathered Elsewhere

And what of our loyal Pakistani ally? How nice of them to help the North Koreans with nuclear weapons. He needed the money, you see.

April 13, 2004

Dr. Rice admits that things are getting complicated. The enemy, the CIA, of my enemy, the FBI, is my totally good buddy. And who was that masked man?

April 13, 2004

Slowly but surely, US casualties start to mount.

April 14, 2004

Soldiers who have finished one tour are extended. At home enlistment figures weaken.

The administration hears calls for a draft. It secretly orders local boards to get organized.

April 21, 2004

Meanwhile in Britain, our ally, the Blair government, goes looking for a new constituency.

April 21, 2004

Former football star Pat Tillman is killed in Afghanistan. Even before it is revealed that he was shot by friendly fire, the press is on the case.

April 25, 2004

17

Fierce fighting in Fallujah ends inconclusively.

April 28, 2004

And just when we're already up to our asses in alligators, the Abu Ghraib photographs find their way to the surface.

May 3, 2004

You become the thing you hate.

May 4, 2004

The Pentagon today released this photograph to illustrate that the President is still firmly in control of Secretary Rumsfeld.

DANZIGER

The name "Lynndie England" is now everywhere.

Soldiers charged with torture are immediately sent home.

Questioning PFC Lynndie England

Private First Class Lynndie England is grilled.

May 9, 2004

Mr. Putin Reacts to the Grozny Bombing

Meanwhile, our friend Mr. Putin returns to Grozny with his customary gentle touch.

May 10, 2004

The Russian government starts to resemble its historic forebears.

July 19, 2004

"Events are in the saddle and ride mankind." – Ralph Waldo Emerson

One of Our Prisoners Writes...

"We thought it looked funny, so pictures were taken..."
PFC Lynndie England

Private England's personal photo collection has all sorts of amusing scenes.

May 15, 2004

GIs in Iraq Are Assigned to Drive Halliburton Contractors Around

Halliburton employees are revealed to be making ten times the salary paid
to the American GIs who guard them.

May 17, 2004

In India

Meanwhile, America's technological superiority is slipping away to overseas competitors.

Congressman Eyewax Rhapsodic Delivers a Eulogy

The gentleman is recognized... THANK YOU, MISTER SPEAKER...

TODAY WE ARE FACED WITH THE LOSS OF THE GREATEST OF ALL PRESIDENTS...

... A MAN WHOSE GREATNESS WAS SO GREAT THAT WE WILL NEVER SEE A GREATER...

MAN OR A GREATER PRESIDENT. HOW GREAT WAS HE? WELL...

HE HAD A GREATNESS THAT BRINGS TEARS TO OUR EYES... AND (SOB!)

SO GREAT WAS HIS GREATNESS THAT WE WILL NEVER SEE SUCH GREATNESS...

AGAIN... (SNIFF..) IT IS SAD THAT HIS GREAT GREATNESS, WAS TAKEN FROM US...

IF ONLY WE COULD HAVE FOUND A WAY TO KEEP HIM WITH US SO THAT THE GREAT...

... eh, hold it. The chair would like to ask if the gentleman is saying he might now be changing his vote against **stem cell research**, risking losing the votes of the right-wing loony fringe that provides the Republican majority in the House?

WELL...

NO ONE'S THAT GREAT

DANZIGER

Nancy Reagan comes out in support of stem-cell technology. A fine Republican she turned out to be.

June 8, 2004

The neo-con philosophy starts to look like more con than neo.

June 19, 2004

A little despereately needed comic relief from Libya.

Poor Rush Limbaugh
... facing his third divorce.
Why, he asks in moments
of thoughtful introspection,
do women turn into insane **liberals**
after living with him for a few years
and run screaming
from the house?

And if there ever was a man who needed all-girl bodyguards it is the old Rushster.

June 16, 2004

35

The vice president of the United States tells a United States senator to go do something biologically impossible. Using shorter words, of course.

June 25, 2004

More Than One Thousand Dead

ENOUGH...

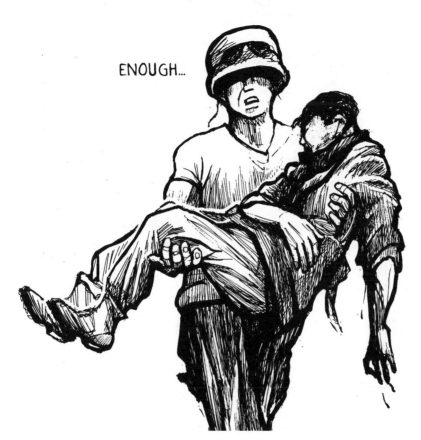

DANZIGER

Mr. Blair cleared, sort of...

EH... THE BUTLER DID IT...

Mr. Blair is exonerated by the Butler Report.

Ariel Sharon Orders All French Jews to Return to Israel

The Israeli prime minister deals with anti-Semitism in Paris by ordering all
French Jews back to the Promised Land. No anti-Semitism there.

Some think things in Palestine couldn't get any worse than they are under Mr. Arafat. Things can always get worse.

July 20, 2004

Television news apparently thinks the war is not its viewers' top priority.

July 28, 2004

In Florida, courts say that felons actually may vote.

With Kofi Annan in Darfur

The UN wrestles with its obligation to do something about genocide, like changing the definition.

Tom Ridge and Friend Visit the Beach

Homeland Security head Tom Ridge warns and warns and warns . . .

Barak Obama is so popular in Illinois you'd have to be crazy to run against him. Fortunately . . .

New York City gets ready to welcome the Republican National Convention right into the belly of the beast.

A hungry world mourns Julia Child.

August 20, 2004

Protests against Bush policies break out in New York City. Central Park is in the spotlight again.

August 21, 2004

In Oslo someone steals Edvard Munch's *Scream*!

August 22, 2004

John Kerry's war record — Silver Stars, Purple Hearts and all — are trashed
by Republican veterans, proving that Vietnam never ends.

August 25, 2004

Actually, no war ever ends.

Ziggy Zell Miller, Democrat turned Bush supporter, threatens everyone including himself. Naturally, we wish him all the luck in the world.

September 7, 2004

As we near the election, Mr. Rove hones the message.

October 5, 2006

Those lucky Afghans!

October 4, 2004

The Pentagon spares us films of wounded American soldiers. Americans might begin to associate war with soldiers getting killed and wounded.

September 30, 2004

Security Mom

Security replaces soccer.

October 7, 2004

Bush assures Americans that the generals get all the troops they ask for.
Later it is revealed that this is untrue.

October 14, 2004

British Troops Replace US Forces Needed for Upcoming Attack

The "special relationship" between the US and the UK takes on a new meaning.

In the last days of the campaign, Senator McCain appears to support the Bush administration.

October 12, 2004

Senator Edwards brings a freshness, a lively sense of youth and hope to the Kerry campaign.

October 3, 2004

The usual guardians of the ballot process.

October 24, 2004

Election Day.

November 3, 2004

Remember: In Iraq and Afghanistan we are fighting theocracies.

November 8, 2004

Bush says he has earned political capital and he intends to spend it.

Dr. Rice is appointed Secretary of State. Colin Powell disappears.

November 16, 2004

Slowly, the world turns.

November 18, 2004

GOP raises the debt ceiling to eight trillion dollars.

Karl Rove — always there when he needs you.

Fighting in Iraq cities intensifies.

November 18, 2004

Mr. Bush stays on-message.

Good Dogs Tommy Franks, George Tenet, and Paul Bremer Get Medals of Freedom

Oddly, Mr. Giuliani, America's mayor, is not incompetent enough to rate a Medal of Freedom.

December 16, 2004

Christmas in the Blue States.

December 23, 2004

Armstrong Williams Won't Return Money He Was Paid to Flak for Bush

Well, then, reasonably, Rush Limbaugh, Sean Hannity, Laura Ingraham, Tucker Carlson, Bob Novak and Oliver North are mad as h*ll!

Mr. Williams was just saying that, as disgusting as it was, a deal was a deal.

At the Inaugural, We're Honoring the Troops

The White House spends millions on the inauguration and dedicates it to our fallen heroes, who are there in spirit.

The Bush Doctrine emerges, this time utterly without checks or balances.

We are faith-based.

January 24, 2005

Iraqi Voters Give Terrorists the Finger

So are the Iraqis.

January 30, 2005

Democrats try to retreat to a place where Howard Dean can't find them.

January 27, 2005

The Clintons agree that if you can't beat 'em, join the church.

February 2, 2005

Christine Todd Whitman, Last Seen at Her Book Party

Christie Todd Whitman, former Republican governor of New Jersey and member of the Bush cabinet, tries to point out some minor disagreements with the Bushies. An example for us all.

January 31, 2005

Meanwhile in Iraq.

January 31, 2005

New York City is perpetually on Orange Alert, and the slightest problem is elevated to a major threat.

January 26, 2005

The Italian government terrorizes itself.

January 20, 2005

Donald Trump gets married again, a triumph of hope over experience.

Social Security Cuts Explained

The Bush administration wants to fix Social Security for people who vote, not for people who will pay.

February 25, 2005

Mr. Frist and Mr. Cheney Hard at Work

Every once in a while, a moderate Republican asks an intelligent question.

February 27, 2005

Navigator Greenspan to Pilot Bush

Mr. Greenspan is not faith-based. To hell with him.

Import controls are taken off textiles. Within days imports surge and more US jobs are eliminated.

March 10, 2005

New Asterisk on Roger Maris' Record *

* Did it without drugs.

DANZIGER

Steroid scandal sweeps baseball.

March 15, 2005

89

Harvard's President Is Envied by All

It is said that the infighting in education is so vicious because the stakes are so small.

What Does Paul Wolfowitz Know About International Finance?

Paul Wolfowitz's incompetence is rewarded.

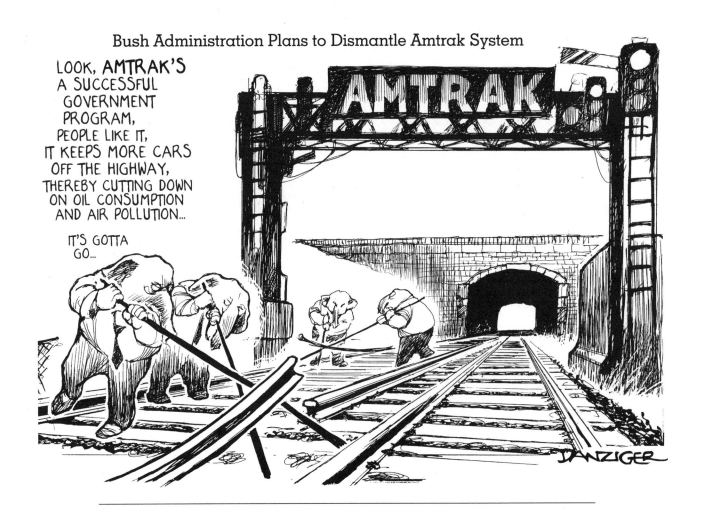

Destruction overseas must be matched by destruction at home. Fair's fair.

March 17, 2005

Faith-based television for Democrats.

A Culture of Respect for Life...

The Republicans redefine themselves . . .

Remember This Poor Guy?

He's an old-style Republican. Good responsible businessman, made the payroll, believed in a day's work for a day's pay, wanted the dollar to be sound, the budget in balance and God in his heaven. Believed in small government and the defense of our borders. Live and let live. Work and save. Privacy... frugality... opportunity...

... that was then...
Good Lord, look at
him now...

... downward.

March 23, 2005

Until the rapture, take a napture.

China Taking Over the Entire World of Apparel Manufacturing

One wonders why they bother to put Made in China on the label any longer.

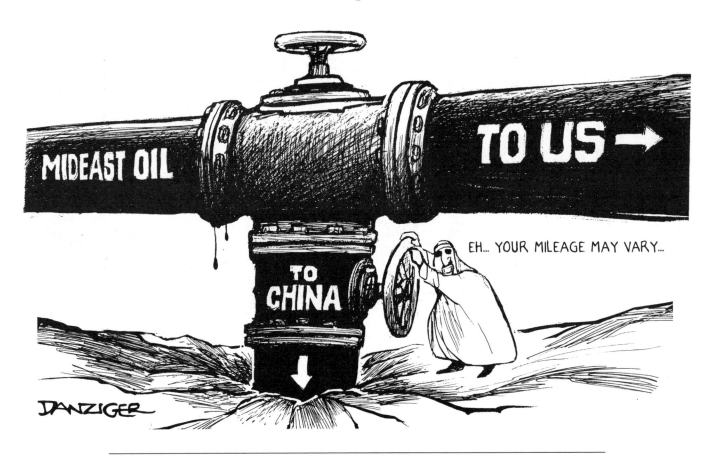

A million more car owners a year.

April 11, 2005

One world, one solution.

March 31, 2005

Got your back, Tom.

Jane Fonda Stops By to Explain Her New Book

She got this idea from Robert McNamara.

Problems of Moral Charity

The disaster in Darfur seeps into the world's consciousness ever so slowly.

The Case of Lynndie England Comes to an End

Tony Blair, in the Last Days of the Campaign

Meanwhile, our ally Mr. Blair approaches another election with his astounding command of the facts. The British electorate has come to loathe him . . .

... which they show by re-electing him.

May 5, 2005

Mr. Hastert Goes Back to the Rule Book. Mr. DeLay is Happy to Help.

Mr. DeLay tries to skirt the requirement that he resign when indicted, a rule
first implemented by Republicans against Democrats.

April 28, 2005

On the Way to Dropping the
Nuclear Option...
Senator Santorum tells
Senator Frist that he is
having second thoughts...

OH, LORD, NOT AGAIN!

DANZIGER

Getting rid of the filibuster, the so-called nuclear option, begins to worry
some Republicans.

April 22, 2005

Cable television news sinks to ever lower depths.

May 3, 2005

Texas Legislature Considers New Rules for Non-sexy Cheerleading

God needs a cheerleading squad if He's gonna win in this world.

May 6, 2005

Laura Bush Says Her Husband Once Mistook a Male Horse for a Cow

LAURA!
TELL HIM!

SOCIAL
SECURITY

DANZIGER

Laura jokes that Bush is quite stupid. She might know something.

But she's still a winning card.

Truth in Labeling

Why we haven't started a war with North Korea.

Check your shorts, too.

May 15, 2005

Newsweek says copies of the Koran were disrespected at Guantanamo Prison. A story too good to check.

May 17, 2005

New Policy from the Vatican: Reaching Out to China, Forgetting Taiwan...

Hate the sin, love the sinner. Love the money, also.

May 24, 2005

After a long nap, Stalin and Lenin are awoken...

Press freedom in Russia — if Putin says it, it's *pravda*.

If you're buyin', they're cellin'.

May 27, 2005

Now you can spend all the time you want with Matt Drudge and Arianna Huffington. For free!

May 25, 2005

TRMPAC (Texans for a Republican Majority)(er... Tom DeLay) Found Guilty

OH, THANK GOODNESS, TOM, YOU'VE BROUGHT ALONG SOME PROTECTION UNTIL I CAN GET BACK ON MY FEET...

NOTHING LIKE LOYALTY AMONG US REPUBLICANS IS THERE?

TRMPAC

DANZIGER

DeLay, who started TRMPAC, pretends he didn't know nothin' 'bout it.

May 27, 2005

Dean told to raise money, not his voice.

June 7, 2005

Army recruiting numbers fall. Even with a multimillion-dollar advertising budget.

June 25, 2005

Gap Widens Between Rich and Poor Under Bush

... WONDER WHAT THE TAXPAYERS ARE DOING THESE DAYS...

MY FAIR SHARE
NEWPORT

The rich don't have to cheat on their taxes anymore. The Bush administration does it for them.

June 6, 2005

The Real Deep Throat

Someone named Mark Felt, now in his dotage, admits he was the Watergate source Deep Throat.

June 1, 2005

Janice Rogers Brown Raised to the Federal Appeals Court

Another brilliant appointment.

Justice O'Connor Retires

The Spureme Court's great swing vote retires.

Dr. StrangeFrist

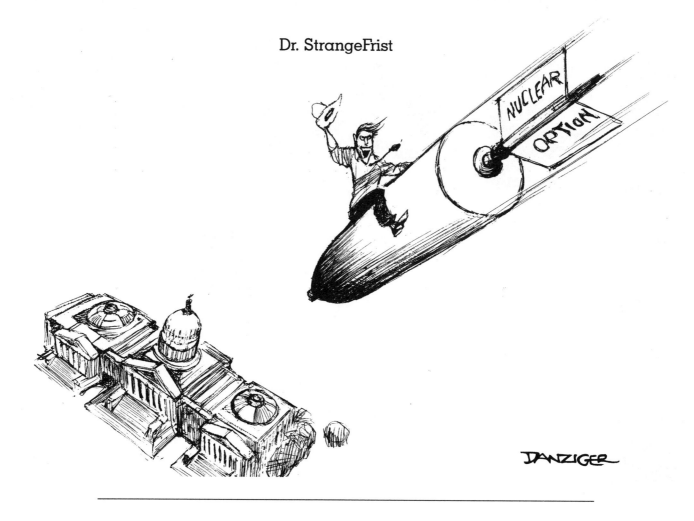

Frist gets closer to bombing the filibuster.

Last Throws from Mr. Cheney

DANZIGER

Which means Cheney will have to cast the deciding vote.

June 26, 2005

In the war news, the "Q" word is heard.

June 27, 2005

Rumsfeld Explains Billion-dollar Shortfall in Money for Vets' Medical Care

And Rumsfeld begins his long descent into the maelstrom.

June 30, 2005

Pope Helping Out in Africa

Of course, about a year later, the pope changed his mind and said that condoms were OK for use in a marriage to prevent transmission of AIDS. Or God changed his mind, or both.

June 13, 2005

Pat Robertson Now Says That Condoms Are OK

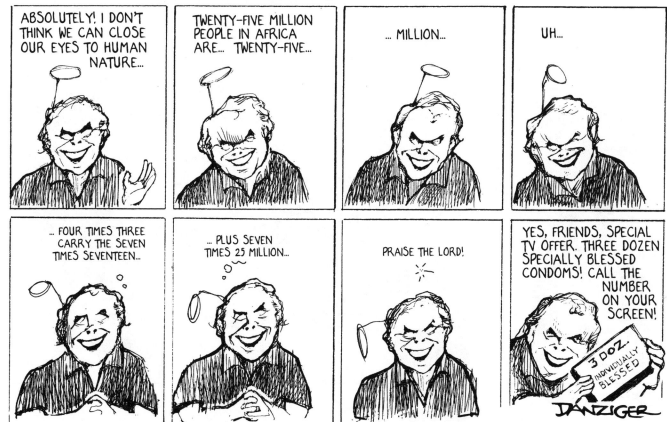

And if there's dollar to be made, can Pat Robertson be far behind?

London Celebrates Winning 2012 Olympics

But the day after this happy announcement . . .

. . . terrorists bombed London, just as they bombed everywhere else.

July 29, 2005

Rove begins redefining victory in Iraq.

July 19, 2005

Karl Rove Explains

Ms. Coulter later apologized, blaming her attacks on the phase of the moon and her need for the money...

John Roberts, a reasonably moderate conservative judge, is nominated to replace Justice O'Connor.

July 20, 2005

Heroes are made, not born.

But the IRA did not forswear step-dancing musicals, and other forms of torture.

July 29, 2005

Senator Santorum attributes all, or most, of the evil in the world to the city of Boston.

August 3, 2005

The law now is basically, "Do whatever you want . . ."

August 8, 2005

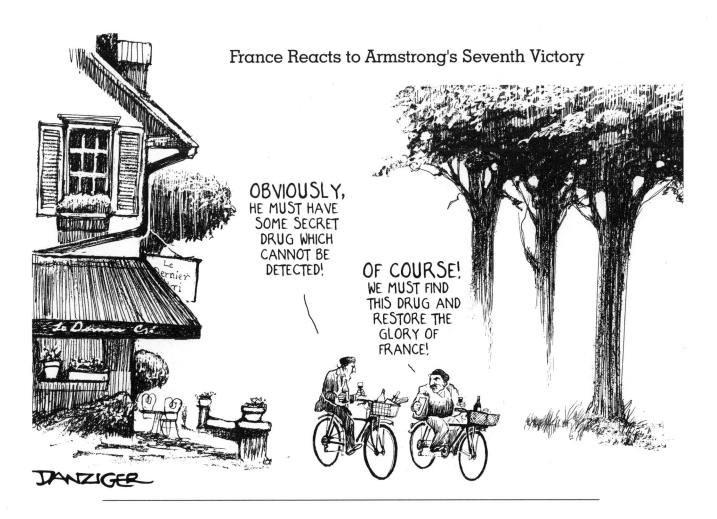

The phenomenon of Lance Armstrong rankles the Gallic soul. Good.

July 6, 2005

August is the cruelest month. Actually they're all pretty cruel.

Look On The Bright Side

Slowly it dawns on Americans that something is wrong with everything being made in China. What could it be? Hmmm . . .

August 15, 2005

The Chinese government tries to rein in the Internet.

August 20, 2005

The Reverend Pat Robertson's Plan to Save Us from Venezuela

Pat Robertson says kill Hugo Chavez. Then he says he's sorry. Or is out of ammunition.

August 23, 2005

Considerable Unhappiness with the Base-Closing Report

We've got to keep Republican districts safe from Godless communism!

War, Famine, Pestilence and Death
Now Joined by the
Fifth Horseman of the
Apocalypse

NO BID
GOVERNMENT
CONTRACTS

War spending drives the deficit to alarming levels.

September 27, 2005

Suddenly the illegal alien, known but ignored for decades, becomes a hot button issue.

August 30, 2005

More Than 1800 US Killed in Iraq War

White House says Bush passed his physical exam with flying colors. In other news . . .

August 2, 2005

And now for the kindness of strangers...

Survival of the Fittest

This call to sacrifice lasts about two days. Then back to shopping.

September 27, 2005

Bush Republicans Heed the President's Call to Conserve Fuel...

Few notice that Hummer rhymes with dumber.

At the Vietnam Wall

History doesn't repeat itself, Mark Twain said, but it rhymes.

Bedtime Stories

Numbers come out of the Pentagon and White House that are later proved to be purest fiction. In war the first casualty is truth. And the second and the third . . .

October 6, 2005

Bush nominates poor Harriet Miers to replace William Rehnquist. She thinks
Bush is the most brilliant man she's ever known, an opinion that should have
disqualified her right off.

October 4, 2005

Mr. Bush Considers Whom to Appoint to Replace Alan Greenspan
on a Thoughtful Walk with His Dog Barney, when suddenly...

And whom shall we get to replace Alan Greenspan?

October 5, 2005

New German Chancellor Angela Merkel
Celebrates the Formation of Her
Coalition Government

WAIT!
THAT MIGHT BE
OUR NEW
EDUCATION
MINISTER...

Germany elects a woman to replace Gerhard Schroeder. But there are two things you don't want to see. One is how German majorities are put together.

October 11, 2005

The trial of the century starts. OK, the fiasco of the century.

October 19, 2005

Fears that global warming is causing endless rain in New England followed
by . . .

October 14, 2005

Hurricane Katrina Refugees in New England Learn About Their New Home

... heavy snows. Well, heavier than ever seen in Louisiana.

October 28, 2005

Mr. Rove and Mr. Libby Show the Administration's Solidarity

Back at the White House, the famed staff solidarity shows signs of fraying.

October 20, 2005

Follow That Scooter!

Never trust anyone with a nickname sillier than Vespa.

Finally someone says something about the Democrats.

Well, the Dems aren't taking this lying down. Just sitting down.

Mt. Chalabi

Ahmad Chalabi, the man whose lies started the war, is put in charge of Iraq's oil industry.

November 13, 2005

God always answers prayers. Sometimes the answer is no.

Rumsfeld advises Hu Jintao.

October 20, 2005

Everyone denies the existence of a CIA prison gulag in the former states of the Soviet Union. Which means it absolutely true.

November 13, 2005

At least Putin has the decency not to put the statue in Lubyanka Square.

November 20, 2005

Midnight in Moscow... again.

Mr. Putin Moves
To Control
All Political
Organizations

But the Russians can't let go of the old KGB tactics.

House Republican Leaders Apologize
After Rep. Jean Schmidt (R-Ohio)
Calls Jack Murtha a "Coward"

AND YOU HAVE NO IDEA
HOW BRAVE I WAS
TO DO THAT...

GOP

DANZIGER

Later it turns out that Ms. Schmidt, tack-sharp as usual, wasn't even aware
that Murtha had been in the service.

November 20, 2005

Walking Point

Mr. Cheney supports the troops at a series of fund-raising dinners.

November 22, 2005

Katrina Relief Stalls

Katrina relief waits while various bureaucracies blame each other.

December 1, 2005

Alaska's Senator Ted Stevens Explains His Unique Patriotism

SCREW LOUISIANA...

Stevens holds out for the famous "bridge to nowhere" in Alaska.

October 25, 2005

It is discovered that Iraqi journalists will lie for money. Heavenly days!

December 2, 2005

In war there's tactics and strategy and retirement . . .

December 4, 2005

Not enough Joe-mentum.

Not Mushrooms Again!

The White House fears that people may be getting bored with Iraq.

December 21, 2005

For a brief moment, it looked like Colin Powell might actually speak the truth.

December 27, 2005

Attorney General Gonzales Says
It's Fine for the Administration
to Spy on Americans Without
Court Orders

AND YOU KNOW WHAT?
J. EDGAR HOOVER WAS RIGHT...
THIS IS MORE FUN
WEARING LADIES'
FRILLY PANTIES!

GET LOST

DANZIGER

There's something about the domestic spying business that makes you want
to dress up in ladies' clothes.

December 28, 2005

Christmas break. Congressmen go home to face the voters, those morons.

December 21, 2005

Mr. Abramoff On His Way to the Prosecutor's Office

We start the new year with Jack Abramoff giving new meaning to a crude
old Washington metaphor.

January 9, 2006

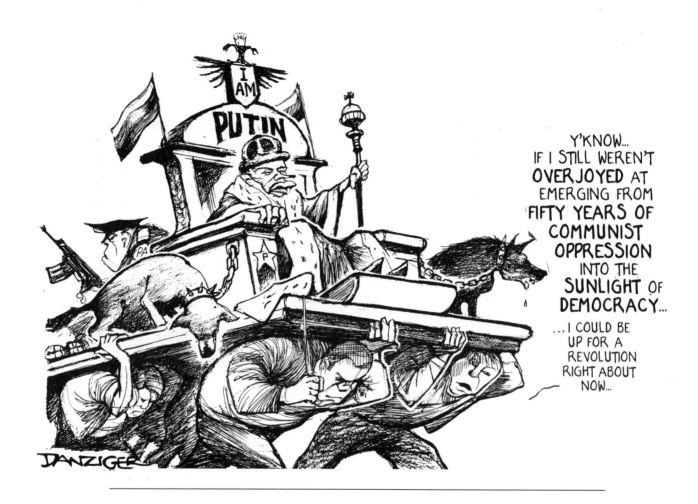

Why be an annoying former Communist when, with a little effort you can be a really loathesome sonofabitch.

January 1, 2006

You have a choice. You can live or you can die.

At least someone will miss printed newspapers.

Another mining disaster illustrating the true cost of coal.

January 4, 2006

The usual suspects.

Pat Robertson's effect on us ink-stained secular humanists is profound!

Another Day in the Bush Administration

PHOTO OP FOR THE PRESIDENT

FUND RAISER FOR THE VICE-PRESIDENT

POLITICAL MEETING FOR DENNIS HASTERT

IMPORTANT MEETING FOR CONDOLEEZZA RICE

SNIPER'S BULLET FOR AMERICAN SOLDIER

ROUND OF GOLF WITH GENERALS FOR DON RUMSFELD

DANZIGER

The main thing is that we never let the terrorists see us worried. Just act natural, as if everything was going just fine.

January 10, 2006

New Challenges for K Street Lobbyists

Jack Abramoff? The names rings a distant bell.

Mrs. Alito Weeps At Sam's Confirmation Hearings

Television gets the important story. A woman is crying.

Sam dimly remembers going to some college that started with a P.

Attack on John Murtha: Same Tactics, Same Flag...

Former marine hero Murtha is attacked by his former comrades-in-arms.

PLEASE WIPE YOUR FEET ↓

THE LAW

DANZIGER

January 18, 2006

195

On the Advice of His Book Publicist, L. Paul Bremer,
Famous Disbander of the Entire Iraqi Army,
Throws His Medal of Freedom
Over the White House Fence.

Bremer's book proves that nothing was his fault.

January 19, 2006

Photos Exist of George Bush Shaking Hands with Jack Abramoff? But Where...?

THE WHITE HOUSE

HEY! YOU WANNA BUY FEELTHY PEEKTURES?

DANZIGER

Go to Photoshop, press "delete."

January 23, 2006

More and more we make less and less.

Production of Winchester Rifles Moves to Japan

KINDA PATHETIC... THIS WAS **THE GUN THAT WON THE WEST,** AND NOW IT'S NOT GOING TO BE EVEN MADE BY AMERICANS...

DON'T WORRY, I CAN GET YOU A JOB PARKING CARS AT THE CASINO...

DANZIGER
AFTER REMINGTON

January 24, 2006

199

YOU CAN NEVER RUN FOR OFFICE, LAURA.
I NEED YOU RIGHT WHERE YOU ARE...

Some talk of Laura Bush running for office is quickly ended.

January 20, 2006

At Home With the Cheneys

Uncle Dick checks on the Google thingy to make sure no one is downloading yucky bad sex stuff...

...meanwhile, Lynne Cheney scopes out some hot babes in action to inspire her next yucky bad sex novel...

DANZIGER

Well, if you were married to Dick, you'd hallucinate, too.

January 23, 2006

201

Justice Alito Confirmed

The Bush Supreme Court takes shape.

Justice Scalia Skipped Chief Justice Roberts' Swearing-in For Tennis Date

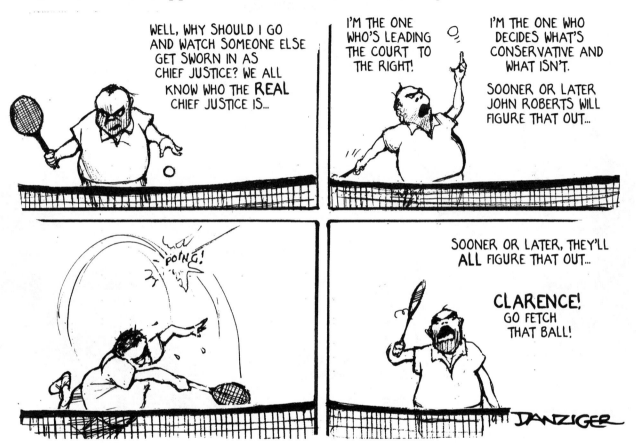

Career Counseling

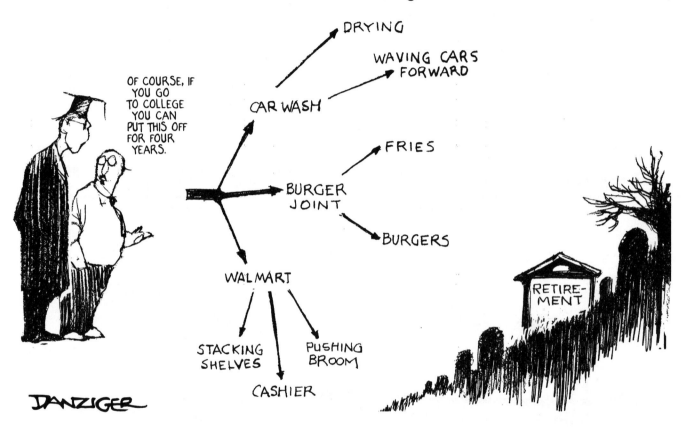

Do you like to work with people?

Laid Off from the Auto Industry? Don't Worry. There's Work for Everyone.

You ever wonder why they keep those guys in the back out of sight?

Everything Else Is Going So Well, Dr. Bush Will Take Care of Your Health Problems

Our plan: Don't get sick.

BETTER THAN
ROCKS, I GUESS...

DANZIGER

Some hope for peace when Hamas wins an election.

January 26, 2006

But things revert quickly to form.

January 31, 2006

Mrs. Merkel Is Told of Iran's Nuclear Threat

W explains the obvious threat to civilization.

January 13, 2006

Mrs. Merkel Says Iranian Leader is a Nazi

Angela goes him one better!

Way ahead of the mullahs, Rumsfeld is hurt by Tom Toles.

February 3, 2006

John Boehner Reassures His Old Girlfriend Kay Street

HEY, BEAUTIFUL...

HEY, HANDSOME...

Boehner takes over for the ailing Tom DeLay. Just temporary, you understand.

February 3, 2006

All Danes must die!

Muslim Cartoonist Gets Advice from His Editors on Caricature of George Bush

The Ghost Walks!!

We sometimes forget Dick Cheney's service in the Nixon administration.

February 6, 2006

Horrible Rumors that Donald Trump Only Has Millions, Not Billions

Trump actually threatened to sue over this horrid insult.

February 6, 2006

Mortgage the future. That's what the future is for.

In China, an Editor is Beaten to Death by Police for Criticizing the Government

OLD CHINESE PROVERB:
NO NEWS IS
GOOD NEWS...

DANZIGER

There is no First Amendment in China. Actually, there are no amendments
at all.

February 9, 2006

And then there are some days when cartoonists wake up and discover they've done our job for us.

February 13, 2006

Dispatches

It may have been a disaster for Cheney's "friend" but it got everyone's mind off the war.

February 14, 2006

In Texas

The Texas mystique never fails to amuse.

When Cheney Goes Hunting, It's a Federal Program

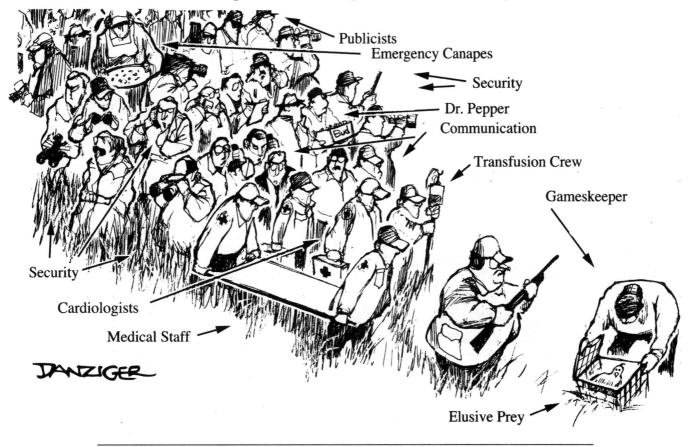

The National Guard

February 17, 2006

223

The Youth of India and America Explain the iPod...

ANALOG AND DIGITAL FILES ARE STORED IN BINARY SIGNALS IN MULTI-LEVEL ROM CHIPS IN Q-342 CODE MASTER BAND 64-BIT DUAL RETRIEVE NON-LINEAR HETERODYNE KEYSTREAM M-CLIP AUDIO FUNCTIONS.

IT'S SO COOL. YOU LIKE PUSH THE BUTTON AND ALL YOUR LIKE MUSIC IS THERE LIKE IF YOU GO TO THE MALL OR LIKE WHEREVER...

DANZIGER

Our only hope is educating Indians in American schools.

Bird Flu in Germany! Government Orders ALL CATS MUST STAY INDOORS!

At least someone is taking the bird flu epidemic seriously.

March 2, 2006

How You Can Enjoy the Winter Olympics at Home

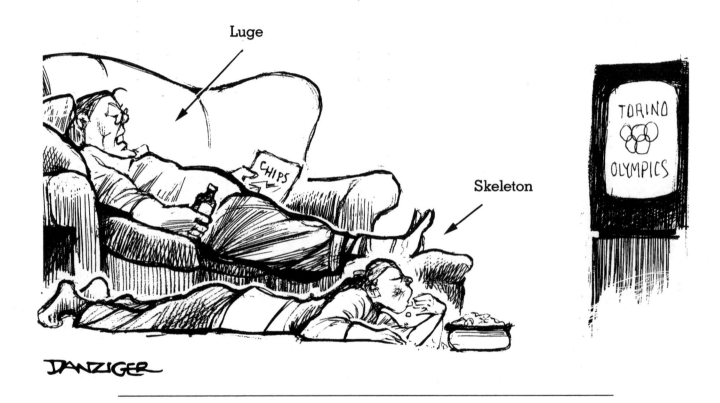

Luge

Skeleton

TORINO OLYMPICS

DANZIGER

If it's downhill, the American public is on board.

In Ratings War, Even Curling Tries to Modernize

As if curling weren't exciting enough.

Dubai Government Cuts Deal to Take Over US Ports

We terrorized those Dubai boys right back! Hah!

Any Port in a Storm

No one can figure out what the administration is up to, but we know we don't want it.

Whither Neo-Conservatism

Messrs. Fukuyama, Kristol and Buckley Discuss the Future of History

Stars of neo-conservatism whisper "my bad."

Karl Rove Said to be Obsessing Over Hillary Clinton

HILLARY '08

GEORGE? YOU ALL RIGHT?

DANZIGER

Bush realizes he has to get rid of his brain.

March 1, 2006

Hillary Has Always Been Against the Dubai Deal, Even When Bill Started It

Hillary wonders Dubai or not Dubai. That's the question.

March 5, 2006

Condi's Workout Philosophy

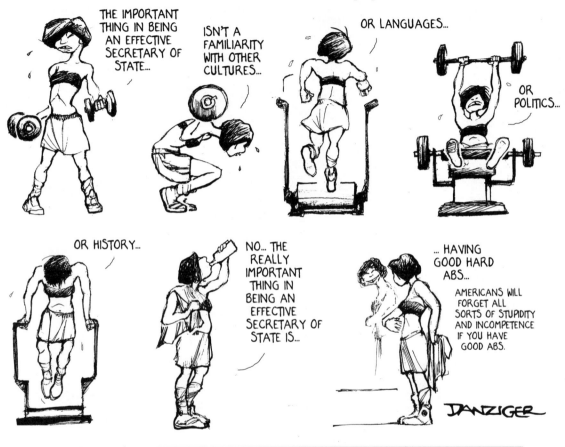

Through it all, Dr. Rice manages to fight the bulge.

George and Barbara's Exit Plan

In fact you can blame it all on Jesus.

Treasury Secretary Snow Suggests to His Staff that the Administration Might Balance the Budget by Borrowing from Government Employees Pension Funds

Well, we'll just have to print some more money with Mr. Snow's name on it.

Hillary now portrayed as angry, the new code word for "unstable."

March 7, 2006

Many aliens from Mexico have excellent credit ratings.

March 8, 2006

237

But Who Can Take Over US Ports If We Fire Those Dubai Boys?

China Still "Harvesting" Transplant Organs from Executed Prisoners

We use everything but the squeal.

And we were worried about American youth.

The Modern American College Student

Polls show that 68 percent of Americans between the age of 18 and 24 can't find Iraq on a map.

March 20, 2006

THE CHICKEN SPECIAL IS
POLLO DE SEGURIDAD..
A CHICKEN BREAST IS MARINATED IN SULFURIC ACID,
RUN OVER BY A TRUCK, MACHINE-GUNNED
AND IRRADIATED OVERNIGHT. THEN SPICED
WITH BOTOX AND INCINERATED IN AN
INDUSTRIAL TEMPERING OVEN.

IT TASTES AWFUL,
BUT YOU WON'T
GET AVIAN FLU
FROM IT...

The fear of bird flu spreads.

March 21, 2006

242

And the birds aren't too happy about us.

March 29, 2006

243

Able Seaman John McCain

WE HAVE TO STAND BEHIND THE PRESIDENT.

AFTER ALL, HE IS OUR LEADER.

HE'S LIKE THE CAPTAIN OF A SHIP...

HE CHOOSES THE COURSE WE'RE GOING TO TAKE.

AS MEMBERS OF THE CREW WE MUST HAVE CONFIDENCE THAT THE CAPTAIN IS CAPABLE AND COMPETENT.

ONLY THEN CAN WE HAVE A SUCCESSFUL VOYAGE...

AND THAT'S WHY I SUPPORT THE CAPTAIN.

I'LL BE ON THE POOP DECK IF ANYONE NEEDS ME...

Danziger

John McCain realizes that if he wants the Republican nomination he has to start hanging around with Republicans.

March 12, 2006

Torture

DANZIGER

What's Good for GM is Good for the Country

Where's Charlie Wilson now that we'd really like to kick his tires?

March 23, 2006

Sweet Dreams

Dick says he only wants fair and balanced news.

March 27, 2006

The number of illegal immigrants is estimated at twelve to fifteen million, or the population of Texas, which it probably is.

March 27, 2006

Andrew Card Realizes That This is His Stop

Andrew Card, who has been with the administration since the beginning, leaves to spend more time with his family, or pursue other career options, or something.

March 28, 2006

Texans Struggle to Make Sense of DeLay's Departure

Ah, the Texas roadhouse again.

We have to protect ourselves from these insane people.

March 24, 2006

CBS Actually Had Tried to Make Over Bob Schieffer

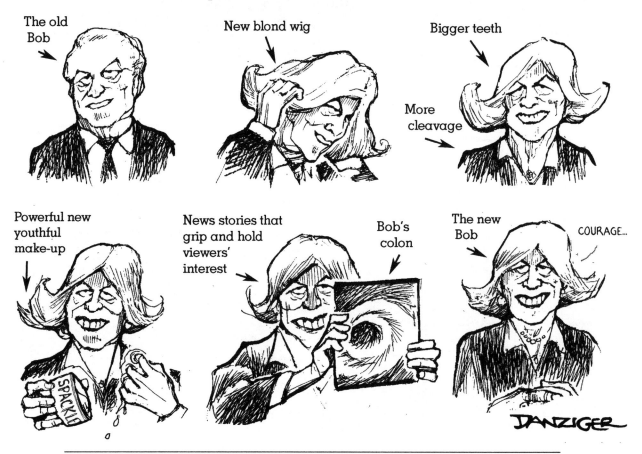

The old Bob

New blond wig

Bigger teeth

More cleavage

Powerful new youthful make-up

SPACKLE

News stories that grip and hold viewers' interest

Bob's colon

The new Bob

COURAGE...

DANZIGER

Katie Couric is CBS's choice to replace Bob Schieffer, who was dangerously increasing viewership of the *CBS Evening News.* We'll put a stop to that!

April 5, 2006

Duly-elected Iraq Prime Minister Ibrahim al-Jaafari Gets Taken for a Ride

Once again, democracy's mistakes have to be corrected by people who have shown they know how to run the world.

April 6, 2006

M.Chirac Orders Champagne

In a bid to make the rest of us feel better, the French act crazy.

Italian Politics

DANZIGER
NYTS/CWS Apr 11 2006 (2750)

By a narrow margin Prodi beats Berlusconi. Outside of Italy, no one cares.
Inside Italy, Berlusconi cares.

April 11, 2006

Another General Retires

I'D LIKE TO STAY, BUT I HAVE A CONTRACT TO WRITE A BOOK ABOUT WHAT A JERK YOU ARE...

It turns out the only one in the Pentagon who can't write is Rumsfeld.

April 11, 2006

New Medals Announced

The Purple Ear
Awarded for Advanced Listening to Rumsfeld's Speechs, Briefings, Rants.

The Brown Star
For Loyalty Above and Beyond Logic. Worn on End of Nose.

The Distinguished Agreement Medal
For Going Along to Get Along

The Congressional Medal of Blindness
For Heroic Lack of Oversight at the Highest Levels

The Double Cross
For Not Writing Book Slagging War Until Safely After Retirement

The Marine Special CocaCola Bottle Bottom
For Fighting On In a War Even the Marines Are Starting to Doubt

The Vietnam Era Shorttimer Medal
Left Over from 70's...
...thousands of them, May amuse children.

The Other Purple Ear
Take a guess...

DANZIGER

Oh, what tangled webs we weave when . . .

. . . eh, we start wiretapping our fellow Americans without warrants.

Scandal Hits Rupert Murdoch's New York Post

IT'S A LETTER FROM SOME DOPEY CARTOONIST, OFFERING TO KEEP YOU OUT OF UNFLATTERING CARTOONS FOR A MERE HUNDRED GRAND DOWN AND TEN GRAND A YEAR...

NY POST GEPHARDT WINS!

DANZIGER

Things go crazy at the *New York Post* . . .

April 12, 2006

Poor John Podhoretz

Just as his book slagging Hillary Clinton comes out,
his boss, the fun-loving Rupert Murdoch, decides
to back Hillary for President.

ACTUALLY, JOHN, I HAVEN'T READ YOUR BOOK...
FICTION IS IT?

DANZIGER
NYTS/'CWS MAY 9 2006 (2781)

. . . and publisher Rupert Murdoch decides to go crazy along with them. He
backs Hillary Clinton.

May 9, 2006

261

The administration entertains the thought of little nukes.

Blair Says Brits Won't Be Going to Iran (Oh, to stay in England now that April's here...)

Tony Blair says God has told him, well, suggested strongly, that he not join Bush in invading Iran.

April 17, 2006

April 17, 2006

Oil hits seventy dollars a barrel.

April 21, 2006

New White House Staff Chief Bolten Calls In Harriet Miers

HARRIET, REMEMBER HOW THE WHITE HOUSE TRADED ON YOUR UNQUESTIONING LOYALTY AND THEN TOSSED YOU TO THE WOLVES WHEN THE GOING GOT ROUGH?

WELL, THE PRESIDENT WANTS TO TAKE ADVANTAGE OF YOUR VALUABLE EXPERIENCE AGAIN...

The former Supreme Court nominee is shown the gate.

April 22, 2006

266

Mr. Hu Reflects on His Trip to the United States

 NATURALLY, I FOUND THE WHITE HOUSE VERY IMPRESSIVE.

 BUT...

 ...BILL GATES' HOUSE...

 NOW **THAT** WAS A HOUSE!

DANZIGER

The Chinese Chief of State comes to the United States. His first stop is Bill Gates' house. And then Washington if he can squeeze it in.

April 23, 2006

MAO WAS RIGHT:
POLITICAL POWER **DOES** GROW
FROM THE MOUTH OF A GUN
AND THE PRICE
iS RIGHT, TOO.

MADE iN CHINA

MADE iN CHINA

DANZIGER

Guns get cheaper.

April 30, 2006

The illegal immigration problem appears to have no good solution, only plenty of lousy ones.

May 9, 2006

Forgotten almost completely is that illegal aliens are also . . . uh . . . you know . . . human beings.

The idea that there is such a thing as too much profit amuses some.

April 25, 2006

The Patriot

Some sneaky pinko from South America somewheres tries to give cheaper oil to poor Americans. We're too smart to fall for that trick.

May 4, 2006

James Baker Called In To Help Fix Bush War Strategy

FINE, FINE... JUST SO ALONG AS
YOU AGREE THAT:
1. I AM A GENIUS
2. I AM A WAR PRESIDENT
3. I NEVER MAKE MISTAKES
4. I AM THE DECIDER

I AM DOING A HECK OF A JOB

DANZIGER

It turns out that there are some disasters even Jim Baker can't fix.

April 24, 2006

Meanwhile, the rest of the world has its own little problems, like chick lit writers lacking originality, if you can imagine such a far-fetched idea.

April 27, 2006

Russian birth rate falls. Soon the world may be out of Russians. And there's bad news!

The Spirit of Two Thousand Six

In this world if you've got oil, you've got friends.

Mr. Hastert Sets an Example for Us All
by Driving... oh, maybe 200 Feet in
a New Hybrid Car.

He then drove
his own car
home.

There's just some rule that fat white guys drive big wasteful cars.

The "sour" mood just showed up out of nowhere.

On the Border

Bush promises six thousand National Guard troops to guard the Mexican border. No one is happy about this.

May 17, 2006

The Grapes of Confusion

Can you say Bienvenidos?

Food Aid to Darfur Cut in Half

A flood of arms. A trickle of humanitarian aid.

Our troops have had enough.

May 7, 2006

May 17, 2006

CIA Scandal Widens to Include Traditional Elements

SORRY LADIES, BIBLE STUDY HAS BEEN CANCELLED...

CIA HOSPITALITY SUITE

DANZIGER

Well, Duke Cunningham was "randy."

May 7, 2006

Giuliani Stumping for Ralph Reed

In the strange bedfellows file, Ralph Reed's run for Georgia lieutenant governor needs a northeastern liberal with shaky moral credentials.

May 22, 2006

Congress tries to give everyone $100 to somehow ameliorate high gas prices.
That doesn't work, but the basic idea has a certain inane appeal.

May 25, 2006

In an Act of Retribution FBI Searches Hastert's Office

So far they're uncovered
4 boxes Chips Ahoy
6 Packages Fig Newmans
1 Happy Meal (Partial)
3 Quarts Fanta Orange
Remains of a Whopper with Cheese
5-lb tub Sam's Club Pretzels
1 Rotisserie Chicken
   (Extra Spicy)
Emergency Bratwurst

Mr. Hastert objects to the FBI searching the Capitol offices.

May 25, 2006

Evidence mounts that few Americans are listening to Bush anymore.

May 30, 2006

Are Haditha Killings a Modern Day My Lai?

Marines shoot civilians in Iraq village, including women and children and an old man in a wheelchair.

May 31, 2006

Ms. Couric Tearfully Leaves Today for CBS News
(Making one little stop along the way.)

Ms. Couric will add her special perkiness to CBS news reports about war,
murder, starvation, and widespread depression.

June 1, 2006

The administration is playing money politics with Homeland Security funds.
Why is no one surprised?

June 2, 2006

In an act of towering maturity, Bush won't talk to the new leader of Iran.

A Threat to the Nation!

IT'S **TRUE!** THIS MORNING WE GOT UP AND WE DIDN'T KNOW WHETHER WE WANTED TO BURN THE FLAG OR GET MARRIED!

LUCKILY, THERE WAS A SECURITY CAMERA WATCHING US OR HEAVEN KNOWS **WHAT** WE WOULD HAVE DONE!

DANZIGER

In the middle of the war, the Senate leadership spends days talking about same-sex marriage and flag-burning. Neither discussion results in legislation.

June 5, 2006

Canada discovers that no pleasant, tolerant, friendly, welcoming policy goes unpunished.

June 6, 2006

Fortunately the "death tax" didn't die . . . yet.

Al-Zaquari dies . . . two cheers.

Brits Told They Must Be Much Better Behaved at the World Cup

The normally thuggish British fans are told they must behave during World
Cup games in Germany. And above all . . . eh . . . don't mention . . . the war..

June 13, 2006

Incredible Pollution. Made in China. Exported Everywhere.

China's increasing soft coal burning spreads soot and sulfur world wide.

June 12, 2006

Karl Rove's "Beat the Rap" Party

Karl Rove told by prosecutors that he will not be indicted. Clink!

Bush notes that as the Iraqis stand up we'll stand down. With some exceptions.

June 13, 2006

LOOK AT THIS! ANOTHER BLATANT ATTEMPT TO ATTACK THE UNITED STATES!

HA! CAUGHT IN THE ACT OF ASYMMETRICAL WARFARE

NOW WE'RE NEVER LETTING YOU OUT!

PUBLIC REACTION

DANZIGER

Guantanamo commander says prisoners hanged themselves just to embarrass the United States. These people are clearly a threat!

June 12, 2006

Ann Coulter Born Again

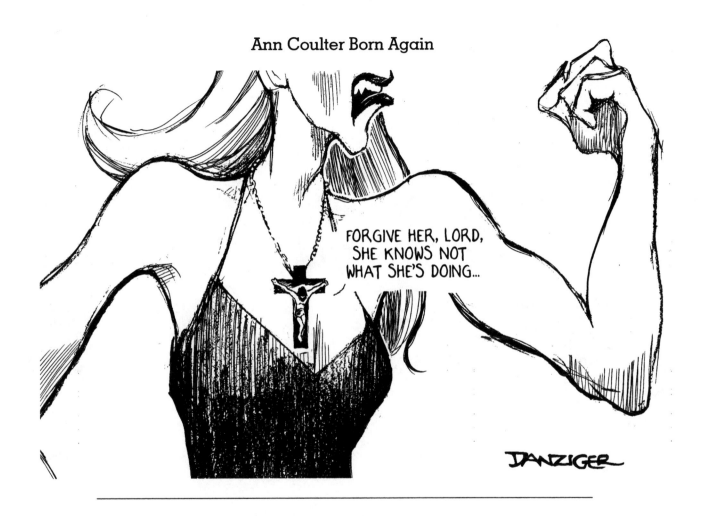

Ann Coulter promotes her new shriek wearing a crucifix.

June 16, 2006

Fight! Fight! Fight!

Sis, Boom, Bah!

Security Problems In New York Subways
Did Terrorists Plan to Release Poison Gas
in the Uptown Local? Or Was It Merely a
Double Hussein Schwarma Plate With Saddam Sauce
from Akbar's Awful Falafel on 127th Ave?
If You Smell Something, Say Something!

Poison gas threat in New York's underground. Some would say it's always
been there.

June 18, 2006

Why Karl Rove Never Served His Country

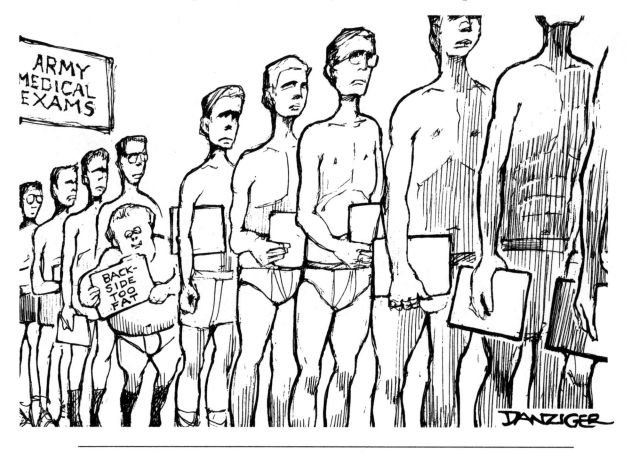

Mr. Murtha accuses Rove of sitting "on his fat backside in his air-conditioned office" while urging others to fight and die.

We await a Democratic victory . . .